Maurice Bloomfield

Historical and critical remarks introductory to a comparative study of Greek accent

Maurice Bloomfield

Historical and critical remarks introductory to a comparative study of Greek accent

ISBN/EAN: 9783337107970

Printed in Europe, USA, Canada, Australia, Japan

Cover: Foto ©Andreas Hilbeck / pixelio.de

More available books at **www.hansebooks.com**

HISTORICAL AND CRITICAL REMARKS

INTRODUCTORY TO A

COMPARATIVE STUDY OF GREEK ACCENT

MAURICE BLOOMFIELD, Ph. D.,

Associate Professor for Sanskrit and Comparative Philology,
JOHNS HOPKINS UNIVERSITY.

REPRINTED FROM AMERICAN JOURNAL OF PHILOLOGY, VOL. IV, WHOLE NO. 13.

BALTIMORE, 1883.

Press of Isaac Friedenwald, Baltimore.

HISTORICAL AND·CRITICAL REMARKS INTRODUCTORY TO A COMPARATIVE STUDY OF GREEK ACCENT.

I.

Accent is a universal phenomenon in language, and one which is in close union with what is treated by grammar under the head of sound or phonology.

The sounds of a word without accent are merely separate stones which accent cements into a linguistic entity, either a word or a sentence. W. v. Humboldt says: ' The unity of the word is produced by the accent. This, by itself, is of a more spiritual nature than the sounds, and it is therefore called the soul of speech, not only because it is really the element which carries intelligibility into speech, but because it is, more than other factors in speech, the immediate expression of feeling ' (cited by Göttling, Accent der griechischen Sprache, p. 8).

The word accent in modern terminology is unfortunately compelled to do duty for more than one linguistic fact. First, in the case of the word, it signifies the *relative* stress and pitch characteristics of its various syllables, with no restriction to that syllable which has the strongest stress or the highest pitch. This is the most scientific function of the word. A closer study of the life of the word cannot be satisfied with a theoretical analysis of its sounds and syllables and a superficial recognition as to which of the syllables has the highest pitch or strongest stress, but it must be known also in *what way* or to *what extent* this syllable is elevated above those surrounding it. Furthermore, the relations of the remaining syllables to one another will always show that the same characteristics which distinguish the tone-syllable κατ' ἐξοχήν attach themselves in a lesser degree to some one or more of the remaining syllables ; in short, I would define word-accent in this wider sense as the history of stress and pitch in the immediate practical subdivisions of the word, its syllables. This definition of accent has necessarily to be kept apart from that other more familiar one by which, in the current parlance of grammar, the pitch or stress of the most accented syllable is designated. This, of course, is not all. For just as the word has its history of pitch and stress, so has the sentence. The members of the sentence stand in a relation to the sentence as a whole which is not unlike that in which the syllables stand to the word. Here, of course, the word 'accent' has again to do double duty: first, it indicates the relative characteristics of the words which make up the sentence, and, secondly, the word is also employed to mark that favored member of the sentence which holds the most prominent position, *i. e.* the one which corresponds to the 'tone-syllable' in the word.

In the sentence 'he did it, not she,' we may speak of accent in its most pregnant sense and refer merely to the two summits 'he' and 'she,' or on the other hand we may call before our minds a picture of the exact relation of each of the words in pitch and stress, not giving our attention merely to the summits, but watching the undulation of the tone-line in which the sentence moves all along, from the beginning to the end. This is the study of accent in its scientific sense.

That the accent of a sentence is as much under the influence of an organic law of some kind as the accent of the word is seen as soon as one attempts to disturb the natural cadence of a sentence such as the one cited above. By transferring the summit pitch and ictus to the second word of the sentence we destroy the organic life of the sentence fully as much as though we change the summit pitch and stress in a single word. 'He *did* it, not she' is as much not an English sentence as '*dé*velopment' is not an English word. Frequently the change of relation in pitch and stress does not go so far as to destroy the sentence, it simply makes another sentence out of it, as for instance when the summit tone is shifted successively from one word to another in the group of words 'give me that book.' We obtain four different sentences corresponding to the four different positions of the summit tone.

With this last case may be compared the way in which, *e. g.* in Greek, the change of accent changes entirely the character of certain words otherwise the same, and in fact enters as a considerably fruitful factor into word-formation. For instance, τροχός is an agent-noun or participial formation meaning 'running,' 'a runner'; τρόχος is an action-noun or abstract, 'a running,' 'a course'; φορός means 'bearing'; φόρος 'a bearing,' a 'tribute'; both couplets are formations identical in every respect but their accent; the accent makes the same phonetic groups into two words as distinctly differentiated in function as two primary noun-formations from the same root can be. And, lest it be suspected that it was merely the superfine linguistic genius of the Greeks which brought in so delicate a factor as a power in word-formation, it may be stated at once that this difference is prehistoric, and Indo-European; the couplet φορός and φόρος makes a perfect proportion with Sanskrit *bharás* 'bearing' and *bháras* 'a bearing,' 'a burden.' In the same manner cf. in Greek μητροκτόνος 'killing his mother' as epithet of Orestes, and μητρόκτονοι 'slain by a mother' as epithet of the children of Medea, the accent alone is the factor which has produced two distinct categories in noun-composition, also prehistoric and Indo-European, and up to date not understood by the familiar guides for the study of Greek.[1]

The chapter on sentence-accent is one of the most difficult and obscure in the study of grammar, and has been brought within the range of scientific discussion only very lately. Of course certain obtrusive phenomena which belong under this head had been noticed and discussed long ago; as for instance the fact that certain words lose their independent accent in the sentence, namely, the

---

[1] Μητρο-κτόνος means literally 'mother-slaying'; it is the kind of compound which is called *tatpurusa* by the Hindu grammarians, that is, a simple compound in which the first member stands to the second in the relation of a case dependent upon it. Μητρό-κτονοι is a secondary adjective compound, what is called in Hindu grammar a *bahuvrīhi* compound, one upon which the idea of possession and the like is secondarily engrafted; the meaning is strictly speaking 'possessing,' *i. e.* being affected by a mother-slaying. The stem κτονο- in the two compounds is not the same; in the first instance it is the nomen agentis κτονός 'slaying,' in the second it is the nomen actionis κτόνος 'a slaying.' The difference of tone in the two compounds represents one of the most noteworthy archaisms in Greek nominal accentuation. Simple dependent compounds like μητρο-κτόνος were originally accented on the second member of the entire compound; this law is so strongly alive in the Greek compounds of this class, whose second member is a noun of agency in -ό-, that the law for recessive accentuation is observed only so far as it does not annul the older law according to which the tone must be on the second member, therefore μητρο-κτόνος is against the recessive tendency. On the other hand, possessive compounds were originally accented on the first member, and in accordance with that, such compounds follow freely the laws of recessive accentuation, as μητρό-κτονοι. The same law reveals itself in such accentual difference as is contained in Sk. *yajñakāmás* 'desire of sacrifice,' and *yajñá-kāmas* 'having desire of sacrifice'; the former is a simple dependent, the latter a secondary possessive compound. The Sanskrit regularly differentiates such compounds by varying accentuation, while in Greek the archaic differentiation of accent is preserved only sporadically. See L. v. Schroeder in Kuhn's Zeitschrift, 101 fg., esp. pp. 106, 110 and 116; Whitney, Sanskrit Grammar, §§1247, 1264 fg. and 1293 fg.

4

enclitics and proclitics ;[1] certain words change their accent according to their position in the sentence: the so-called anastrophe[2] of

[1] That the proclitics do not lack an etymological accent (cf. below, p. 36), but
that they lose their accent from syntactical causes, *i. e.* from their relation to
other words in the sentence, can often be shown easily, either by pursuing their
history within the language itself, or by comparison with corresponding words
in other languages. For instance, οὐ proclitic appears at the end of a sentence
and in some other cases as οὔ; ὡς and ἐξ when they follow the governed word
appear as ὥς and ἔξ (θεὸς ὥς, κακῶν ἔξ). That the proclisis of ὁ, ἡ is not due to
some etymological peculiarity of these words is shown by the Sanskrit corres-
pondents *sá, sâ*; οἱ, αἱ the special Greek new formations for older τοί, ταί (Sk.
masc. *té = τοί*) are made analogically after ὁ, ἡ, and borrow from them their
proclisis. In the same manner no doubt all proclitics lose their accent owing
to syntactical relations, *i. e.* their lack of accent is due to Greek laws of sentence
accentuation. About enclisis we will have much more to say below.

[It is almost needless to add that the word 'proclitic' is a modern invention
brought into currency by G. Hermann (Göttling, p. 387). That does not militate
against the existence of the thing ; only there seems to have been no recognition of it in antiquity, and the omission of the accent in the cursive MSS was
due to differentiation, to the desire of distinguishing not only between ὅ and ὁ,
ἤ and ἡ, οἵ and οἱ, αἵ and αἱ, but also between οὐ and οὖ, εἰς and εἷς, ἐν and ἐν,
ἐξ and ἔξ, the *spiritus asper* not being heard at that time. See G. Uhlig, Zur
Wiederherstellung des ältesten Compendiums der Grammatik, Festschrift zur
Begrüssung der XXXVI Philologenversammlung, p. 80.—B. L. G.]

[2] The true explanation of anastrophe is as follows: Originally 'prepositions'
were oftener or as often 'postpositions,' *i. e.* the position of these small words
in the sentence was a free one. This is clear, especially from the Vedic Sanskrit, where some of the most common ones occur oftener after their nouns than
before them (*e. g. ā* 'to' occurs in the Rig-Veda 186 times after its case and
only 13 times before it). The mere fact that in later periods of language (*e. g.*
Greek and classical Sanskrit) the tendency is to place them before their cases
in itself proves nothing against this natural assumption. The case of a monosyllabic preposition like ἐξ, which receives its natural accent after the word it
governs, but is proclitic when it precedes it, points to the probability that the
true accent of these Greek particles must be looked for in their postpositive
position. Indeed, just as ἐξ (orthotone), so do all bisyllabic prepositions appear
with their true accent when they follow their cases, and just like ἐξ (proclitic)
do all bisyllabic prepositions exhibit *a substitute for proclisis* when they accent
their ultimate. The grammars which regard the oxytonesis as the original
accentuation, of course explain it as due to a desire on the part of the language
to point to the word governed by means of the accent, but such an explanation
needs hardly to be refuted.

The originality of the tone of bisyllabic prepositions in anastrophe is proved
in addition by the fact that this accent is demanded by the corresponding
Sanskrit words whenever the etymology is clear. So Sanskrit *ápa* is not to be
compared with Greek ἀπό but with ἄπο; Sk. *ápi* not with ἐπί but with ἔπι; in
the same manner the archaic character of the accentuation in πέρι, πάρα and

oxytone bisyllabic prepositions, which, as is now generally believed, preserves the original accentuation of these prepositions. The change of an acute to a grave on an oxytone before another word, though a phenomenon totally unexplained,[1] contains no doubt a

ὑπο is warranted by Vedic *páti, párā* and *úpa*; the etymology of *μέτα* and *κάτα* is obscure, but they probably, like those preceding, have preserved their original form in paroxytonesis; ὑπερ is not to be directly compared with Sk. *upári*, which is reflected exactly in the oxytone ὑπείρ; ὑπερ may have preserved an originally different accentuation, or it may have followed secondarily the accent of the other prepositions which suffer anastrophe, aided perhaps by the accent of ὑπερος = Sk. *úpara*. On the other hand ἀμφί, which does not suffer anastrophe, is borne out in its oxytonesis by Sk. *abhí; ávrí* to be sure is oxytone after the case which it governs, against the accent of Sanskrit *dnti;* but it may have left the company of the prepositions with anastrophe, because it differs from all of them in having its first syllable long (by position). In fact it appears to be a law, unnoticed even by Benfey, the author of this explanation of anastrophe, that only prepositions of two short syllables are affected by it (ὑπείρ always oxytone, but ὑπερ—ὑπὲρ with anastrophe). The etymology of ἀνά and διά is obscure, but there is again no reason to doubt that their oxytonesis is based on good etymological grounds. The fact that these prepositions were originally paroxytone is proved also by the fact that they are so accented in adverbial function. Prepositions were originally adverbs, which have become attached to certain cases secondarily and in relatively later periods of language. Many common prepositions in Greek are still adverbs in Vedic Sanskrit: *dpa, prd, párā* (ἀπο, πρό, πάρα), while *pári* (πέρι) does function for both; conversely the Vedic *áti* (ἔτι) is both adverb and preposition, while in Greek it has remained adverb only.

The assumption that such accentuation as ἀπό, παρά, etc., contains a substitute for proclisis is easily vindicated. As a matter of fact only monosyllables are toneless in proclisis; the treatment of bisyllabic words in the same position is in perfect accord with the treatment of enclitics when these contain a too great number of morae. Just as enclisis is restricted to three morae and two syllables (therefore λόγος τις, but λόγοι τινές, cf. below, p. 22), so proclisis is restricted to one syllable and two morae (therefore ἐκ πάντων, but περὶ πάντων). The author of this ingenious explanation of anastrophe is Benfey (' Die eigentliche Accentuation des Indicativ Praesentis von ἐς *sein* und φα *sprechen* sowie einiger griechischen Praepositionen,' Göttinger Gelehrte Nachrichten, Febr. 27, 1878, p. 165 fg., reprinted in Vedica und Linguistica, p. 90 fg.); he closes his article with the following remark: " . . . es ist nicht besonders rühmlich für die griechische Philologie, dass, nachdem sie mehr als zwei Jahrtausende mit verhältnissmässig geringer Unterbrechung geübt ist, noch in ihren jüngsten Lexicis und Grammatiken die Formen ἀπό, ἐπί, παρά, περί, ὑπό, κατά, μετά aufgestellt werden, welche in der Sprache weder je vorkommen noch vorkommen konnten.'

[1] An elaborate discussion of this difficult question, which space forbids us to reproduce even in a condensed form, is contained in the essay of Leonhard Masing: Die Hauptformen des Serbisch-Chorwatischen Accents, nebst einleit-

6

difficulty whose solution will depend upon further investigation in sentence-accent. The difference between interrogative and indefinite pronouns (interrogatives, orthotone; indefinites, enclitics) is a case where *sentence-accent*, apparently, has given the language a method for differentiating an originally single category into two; this also is not understood, but the archaic character of this phenomenon is warranted by similar methods in other languages.[1] And it has been urged lately that two different word-forms which perform the same function, may owe their difference in form to different intonation in sentence nexus.[2]

enden Bemerkungen zur Accentlehre des Griechischen und des Sanskrit, St. Petersburg, 1876, p. 19 fg.

[1] The relation of τίς, orthotone and interrogative, to τις, enclitic and indefinite, is evidently the same as that of the German interrogative 'wer' to the indefinite 'wer' in such sentences as the following: '*Wér* ist gekommen?' and ' Es ist wer gekommen.' We recognize at once that the enclisis of the indefinite is due to its peculiarly subordinate position in the sentence and not to any etymological deficiency, it is therefore a feature of sentence-accent. Cf. the still less clear method of the Sanskrit for differentiating interrogatives from indefinites. By various particles (some enclitic and others orthotone : *ca, cand, cit,* etc.) the interrogative without losing its own tone becomes indefinite, thus *kás* ' who?' *káç ca* ' any one'; cf. Lat. *quis* and *quisque,* identical in form and meaning. Whitney, Sk. Gram. §507; Delbrück, Die Grundlagen der griechischen Syntax, pp. 138, 145.

[2] The most striking instance of this kind is an attempt to account for the different forms of the third person plural of the copula. It is true that the various forms of it, Doric ἐντι, Attic εἰσι, Ionic ἔασι, cannot be carried back to any one origin by any phonetic jugglery. Accordingly complicated processes of analogy have been resorted to generally in order to harmonize these forms. Gustav Meyer's view, *e. g.* is that σ-αντι is the Greek 'ground-form.' From this form he derives ἔασι by assuming that the ε was added secondarily from the strong forms of the root (*e. g.* ἐστι) to *σασι for *αντι, *i. e.* *σ-αντι; while Doric ἐντι, Attic εἰσι, are also to be derived from *αντι by assuming that the initial vowel was assimilated to the ε of the strong forms. Others employ other processes of analogy in order to harmonize these forms with one another. But Joh. Schmidt has taught for some years past that Doric-Attic ἐντι—εἰσι is to be referred to a form *σ-έντι (= Germ. s-ind, Zend. h-eñti), while ἔασι is to be referred to *σ-αντι in the manner exhibited above. The two forms *σ-εντι and *σ-αντι are explained as, originally, respectively the orthotone and the enclitic forms of the word in accordance with the ideas of Wackernagel as laid down in Kuhn's Zeitschrift, XXIV, p. 457 fg., cf. below, p. 36 fg. Of these two forms *σ-εντι, the orthotone form, crowded out *σ-αντι in Doric and Attic, while *vice versa* *σ-αντι, the enclitic form, gained the supremacy among the Ionians. This explanation is laid down with a very slight modification in the doctor-dissertation of his pupil, Felix Hartmann: ' De Aoristo Secundo,' p. 68, while

From the first opening out of the accented Vedic texts, a very important fact bearing upon sentence-accentuation had been noticed. In Sanskrit the finite verb in principal clauses is enclitic, while in subordinate clauses it is orthotone; this fact lay fallow until Jacob Wackernagel, in the 23d volume of Kuhn's Zeitschrift, p. 457 fg., showed that the Greek verbal recessive accent is nothing more than this enclisis of the finite verb extended to all kinds of sentences, subordinate as well as principal, but at the same time modified by that peculiar law of Greek according to which enclisis cannot extend beyond three morae. Wackernagel's ingenious discovery we will discuss in full further on; the point which is to be recognized here is the fact that the study of sentence-accentuation is destined to a prominent place in the grammars of the future, and that the present generation of scholars will, beyond a doubt, see this develop into a science; the delicacy of the subject will call for the keenest penetration, but this will be rewarded by the importance of the results; results of comparative grammar alike valuable to the phonetist, the morphologist, and above all perhaps the student of syntax.

The study of accent in these two forms (sentence and word-accent) has then gained a distinct place in grammar. It may be mentioned also that the phonetist recognizes phenomena closely parallel to these in the structure of the syllable. The syllable also has a relative accentuation, *i. e.* its various parts exhibit different degrees of pitch and stress, and like the word the syllable has usually one summit, which is a sonorous element, most frequently a vowel, as *e. g.* in hánd; often a lingual or nasal as in the second syllable of anchŕrite, anglŋg, handsmmmst. That the summit accent is variable in position, according to the character of the syllable, can be readily observed in taking a set of pairs of syllables which vary from one another in their final consonants, these being in the one case surd and in the other sonant: *seed* and *seat, pease* and *piece, brogue* and *broke;* the syllable tone of *seed, pease* and *brogue* is upon a part of the vowel nearer to the final consonant than in *seat, piece* and *broke.* Further, there may, just as in word-accent, be more than one summit-accent, especially in long syllables.

Schmidt himself has returned to the expedient of analogy in KZ. XXV, 591. Hartmann also employs Wackernagel's ideas on sentence-accent in order to explain the various forms of the second aorist, *ibid.* p. 66. And Wackernagel himself (KZ. XXIV, p. 470) accounts for the loss of augment in preterits by assuming different accentuation in subordinate and principal sentences.

If the syllable 'yes' is pronounced in a contemplative way, *e. g.* in the sentence 'yes, that may be so,' it receives two summits with a decided fall between them. In general it can be noticed that in isolated syllables the relative accentuation of the various sounds gains especially clear expression; so *e. g.* in the various uses of the word 'well' in such connections as 'well, let's go then,' and 'well, are you ready?' The first 'well' has falling tone, the second rising tone.

The subject of syllable-accentuation so far has not gained a very important place in grammar, and still belongs to the phonetist rather than to the grammarian. But taken in connection with word and sentence-accentuation, syllable-accentuation serves to show that accent has been and still is a constant factor at work upon every infinitesimal subdivision of human speech. If we imagine the course of human speech represented by a line, this line will be a *constantly* undulating one when we wish to mark the varying pitch of the sounds; if we wish at the same time to convey a picture of the varying stress or ictus the line would constantly and gradually vary in thickness. Add to this the fact that this variation in pitch and stress is not the effect of one single kind of accentuation, but of a threefold one, and it will be understood how delicate a subject for investigation it becomes even in living speech. In dead languages the difficulties are increased so as to make it hopeless that all the bearings of accentuation will ever be understood. The discussion must restrict itself almost entirely to accent in its pregnant sense, *i. e.* what we have termed summit-accent; only rarely will the stations for lower pitch or minor stress play a part in the discussion. For all the tradition on the subject, preserved either in accent marks or in the description of contemporaneous grammarians, is restricted to that, and is very fragmentary, as well as vague in its terminology.

The general phonetic bearings of this subject can at present be studied most conveniently in Sievers's Handbuch der Phonetik (Manual of Phonetics), especially §§32–6, pp. 177–95 (word and sentence-accent) and §§29 and 30 (on syllable tone).

II.

It seems to-day almost a truism to state that a discussion of Greek accent must start from whatever knowledge there is on Indo-European accent; in other words, that the study of Greek accent must be comparative. This is true precisely as much in this division of Greek phonetics as in any other, as for instance the study of Greek consonants, where one would not now-a-days presume to say much without bringing in the related languages. This, however, does not exclude the fact that accent is, more than other factors in speech, subject to those forces in language which produce change. The Greek and Latin three-syllable accentuations present so fixed and peculiar a physiognomy even in their earliest phases that one would suspect that this restriction to the last three syllables of the word is something that was inherent in these languages from their origin, yet it has been proved for the Greek that this extremely peculiar accentuation is a development out of a system of accentuation to which such a restriction was originally totally unknown.

The German language to-day exhibits a seemingly fixed law of accentuation, namely, that of the root-syllable. This seems a reasonable accentuation, for of all parts of a word the root would seem to be the most prominent and therefore entitled to superior stress and pitch. Yet no fact in linguistic history is at present so clear as this, that the original German accentuation was *not* restricted to the root-syllable, but was a free movable accent, often upon the root, but hardly less often upon some suffixal element. This is proved by Verner's law, and the accentuation of the root-syllable in the German of to-day cannot be due to anything else than the analogy of those words which, under the old free tone-law, exhibited the accent on the root; an analogy carried out with almost flawless consistency.

This does not exhaust the variety of accentual methods to which Indo-European languages have arrived by various processes, often very obscure. The Lithuanian division of the Lithu-Slavic family consists of Lithuanian proper, Lettish and old Prussian. The last branch has died out without leaving any tradition as to its accentuation; the first, the Lithuanian, exhibits a free accentuation which can be compared and identified with that of the Vedic Sanskrit, in spite of many deviations. The Lettish, which is related as closely to the Lithuanian as the language of Herodotus is to that of Thucydides, has abnegated all historic accentuation and accents everywhere the first syllable.

We need not go so far as the Lithuanian and Lettish to find an equally striking and equally difficult phenomenon. The Aeolic dialect in Greece is differentiated from the other dialects in that it has given up almost entirely the accentuation of the ultimate. Excepting the oxytone prepositions of two syllables and a few conjunctions like αὐτάρ, ἀτάρ, there can be no accentuation except that of the penultimate and the antepenultimate (Göttling, p. 29). This is one of the main elements in the fabled special resemblance between the Aeolic and Latin, and has been the cause of much nonsense,[1] and this resemblance with the Latin has also given birth to the equally erroneous idea that the Aeolic accent is older than that of the remaining Greek dialects. On the contrary, no one fact in Greek accentuation is clearer than this, that the oxytone words in Greek are generally archaic, that they have more than all others resisted the recessive accent.[2]

To this tendency on the part of accentual systems to change in such a way as to lose its original complexion entirely, the fact is due that the comparative treatment of accent was, until very recently, a method which had not gained a firm hold upon the

[1]All these do not exhaust the varieties of seemingly fixed systems which have been built up upon the debris of the old I. E. accentuation in the various families. In the Slavic languages, the Russian has still preserved noteworthy points of contact with the accented Vedic Sanskrit, but the Bohemian has adopted the same system as the Lettish mentioned above, namely, the accentuation of the first syllable, while the Polish has worked out for itself a still more peculiar system. All its words, excepting those borrowed from adjoining dialects, are paroxytone, and here we are again led to the only reasonable explanation, namely, that the frequent paroxytone accent of I. E. times was here extended into a law.

We can pick a case from the modern Romance dialects which will show the same complete change of accentuation, and which will at the same time carry the solution of the change with it. The words which are the representatives of the old abstract suffix *tāt* (Lat. nom. *tās*, *fraternitas*) are oxytone: French *fraternité*, Ital. *fraternitá;* oxytone accent is a most non-Latin quality. A solution for this case which is altogether probable is that the modern oxytonesis has preserved the accentuation of the oblique cases: *fraternitātis*, etc. The English on the other hand holds to the accent of the nominative. In the same way the French *conscription* has the accent of the oblique case, *-ōnis*. In a case like French *parlér* over against Italian *parláre* the accentuation of the ultima carries its own solution with it still more clearly.

[2]Almost all the important categories of noun-formation which are oxytone appear in their original accentuation, as can be seen even from superficial comparison. Thus nouns of agency in *-ός, φορός* = Sk. *bharás;* but the nouns of action are paroxytone, φόρος = Sk. *bháras;* adjectives in *-ύς, ἡδύς* = Sk. *svādús, ἐ-λαχύς* = Sk. *laghús, ὠκύς* = Sk. *āçús;* adjectives in *-ρός, ἐρυθρός* = Sk. *rudhirás;* verbal adjectives in *-τός, κλυτός* = Sk. *çrutás* = O. H. G. *hlūt* = Eng. *loud* (KZ. XXIII 123), πηκτός = Sk. *paktás;* the word for father, πατήρ = Sk. *pitá* = Goth. *fadar* (ibid. 117); the perfect active participle εἰδώς = Sk. *vidván* (cf. ἰδυῖα = Sk. *vidúṣī*). In declension πούς : ποδός = Sk. *pád : padás;* Ζεύς : Δι(F)ός = Sk. *dyāús : divás.*

minds of investigators. Parallelisms and resemblances between individual facts of Greek and Sanskrit tone-laws were noted very soon; even large collections of words and word-categories which exhibited identical accentuation were made, yet this did not seem to impress investigators with the fact that, unless these resemblances were accidental—and that theory was not advanced—the two languages were committed to the same original accentuation in every part, and that it must be shown why and how they present such important differences in historical times. On the contrary, investigators were content to call in, for Greek as well as Latin, the recessive principle (which after all is not recessive, inasmuch as it stops at the third syllable) as a something gotten no one knows where, perhaps as Bopp has it 'because the greatest recession of tone expresses the greatest dignity and energy.' [1]

To-day any one who wishes for a hearing on the subject of the accentuation of any Indo-European language must operate with the following principles:

1. The accentuation of any I. E. language is a development out of the common I. E. accentuation, precisely as much so as the sounds and forms of that language, be they ever so changed, and be their analysis ever so difficult or even impossible.

2. The principle which changes accent is precisely the same as that which changes other language matter, regular phonetic change based upon phonetic law. Just as an I. E. consonant is changed in German according to Grimm's law, so it is possible that, e. g. originally oxytone word-categories may become paroxytone in some one language,[2] only this must be shown to take place accord-

---

[1] Vergleichendes Accentuationssystem des Sanskrit und Griechischen, p. 16.

[2] Or we will recognize below (p. 22) as important another Greek phonetic law of accent, namely this, that enclisis cannot extend beyond three morae and two syllables. Enclisis in general is an Indo-European quality (e. g. Greek τε = Sk. ca = Lat. que, etc., are all of them enclitic), but the Greek restriction as to morae and syllables is a Greek phonetic law in exactly the same sense as, e. g. the loss of F or I. E. v. The Vedic Sanskrit knows no restriction of this kind; a word of any length may be enclitic, as e. g. the stem sama 'any one' (Greek stem άμο- in άμό-θεν) is enclitic, not only in forms containing two syllables, but in all its forms, e. g. acc. samam, abl. samasmāt, gen. samasya. And several enclitic words may follow one another, so several vocatives, or vocatives with cases depending upon them, as e. g. Rig-Veda, VII 64, 2: á rājāna maha ṛtasya gopā . . . yātam: 'O ye kings, guardians of great right come hither.' Here four successive words are enclitic, cf. Journal of the American Oriental Society, Vol. XI, p. 59.

ing to a law, and this law must like all other phonetic laws be based upon the results of observations exercised upon extensive material.

3. Where no phonetic law can be adduced, the influence of analogy must be the changing factor. So *e. g.* the modern German with its prevailing accentuation of the root-syllable, the significant syllable has been explained above; the influence of analogy in the Greek ' recessive' accent will be discussed further on; it is perhaps the most striking and convincing case of the workings of analogy.

4. The influence of foreign languages and adopted words cannot be left out of account. These usually carry their tone with them from home. So *e. g.* large categories of words in German betoken by their accentuation what is also known otherwise, namely, that they are of foreign descent, *e. g.* nouns in *-tät, -ion,* etc., *universität, institution,* which exhibit foreign accent; the entire class of verbs in *ieren, studieren, marschieren,* in the same manner exhibit French suffix and French accent; according to Grimm words like *reiterei, malerei,* etc., have suffixal accentuation, although they are in their root good German words, because they were formed on the analogy of *melodey* (μελῳδία), *abtei* (abbatía), so that this is an example where a distinct category of German words received both suffix and accent from abroad.[1]

The question which arises next is: What was the character of this Indo-European accentuation from which the various peculiar accentuations of the several languages have developed? Of course the question can be answered only for the smallest part; almost all that is known is restricted to the summit-accent, and even here nothing is absolutely and completely clear. We will here consider only the one fact which, above all others, has gained an unimpugned position, namely, the freedom of position of the summit-tone of the I. E. word; other qualities both of word and sentence-accentuation, which are probably Indo-European, will be discussed further on in connection with the Greek itself.

The fact that the I. E. parent-language knew none of those restrictions as to the position of the tone which we see in almost all the languages that are still alive, and also in Greek and Latin, especially the latter, is seen by a comparison of the accented Vedic

[1] The influence of foreign languages upon accentuation is still more strikingly exhibited in the threefold tone of the German word *grammatik,* namely, *grámmatik, grammátik* and *grammatík.* The last contains the French accent (*grammatíque*), the one preceding the Latin (*grammática*), while the first represents the genuine German pronunciation with the tone on the root.

Sanskrit with the Greek and German. This comparison yields the
result that the Vedic accent has preserved very closely the old
word-accent of the I. E. parent-speech. Of course this result was
obtained by the usual methods of comparison. Whatever in Greek
and German accent has, upon investigation, proved itself to be
archaic, is not only to be found freely in the Vedas, but is usually
seen there in the form of a principle of wider scope. So *e. g.* the
seemingly irregular accent of the participles and infinitives of the
thematic or second aorist in Greek is an archaism on Greek ground.
In the Veda this entire tense-system is accented on the same place,
the thematic vowel, except in the augment forms, where the augment
always takes the tone, cf. below, p. 38. In the same manner it will
be observed repeatedly that the Greek cases of oxytonesis are
usually of a somewhat disjunct and fragmentary character. Not
clear in themselves, they do not yield up any principle until we see
them in their full bearings in the accent of Vedic word-categories
which accent the ultima. And again in German, Verner's law has
shown that the more salient principles of Vedic accentuation, such
as the shifting of the accent from the root to the flexional element
in the non-thematic conjugations, belong to the oldest property of
I. E. speech, cf. below, p. 15, note; it has also shown that apparently irregular accentuations, such as the Vedic accent of the nouns
of relationship, *pitár* but *mátar,* must be carried back to the primitive Indo-European language.

No syllable, then, of an I. E. or Vedic word was, on account of its
position or on account of its quantity, unable to bear the summit-
tone ; no restriction, such as is seen in the three-syllable accents of
Latin and Greek, or in the root-accent of the German, is to be
found. Thus *índra, índreṇa, ánapacyuta, ánabhimlātavarṇa, ag-
nīnām, abhimatiṣāhā, parjányajínvita,* etc. (Whitney, Sk. Gram.
§95) present instances of Vedic accentuation. As far as the meaning
and value of this free accentuation is concerned, it must be confessed
that little or nothing is known. Indeed, it may be fairly said that,
in accordance with the more modest spirit in which linguistic
investigation is carried on to-day, no very ardent search is made at
present for a cause which distributes the accents over these various
syllables. It is felt generally and justly that final explanations of
such delicate questions are not in order. The energy of accent-
investigators must be directed to an investigation of the simple
details of accentuation, and the causes of these variations in the
separate languages, before it can be hoped at all that the original

cause of these phenomena will be understood. As long as *e. g.* the restriction of Latin accent to penult and antepenult is a mystery, so long there can be no hope of actually penetrating into the inner life of the accentuation which preceded it.

Yet a noteworthy attempt to explain the I. E. accentuation dates back to 1847. The first one and almost the last one who undertook to describe, systematically, the accent in its historical development in the I. E. languages, and at the same time to assign a cause for its original character, was a French scholar, Louis Benloew, in a work entitled ' De l'accentuation dans les langues indo-européennes tant anciennes tant modernes.' According to Benloew the summit-accent was originally an accent purely of pitch, a musical accent without stress or ictus. In each word which consisted of more than one syllable, some one syllable was pronounced musically higher than all the others; the syllable which was thus distinguished from the others was, according to Benloew, the chronologically last defining element in the word (le dernier déterminant). That is, according to the theory of word-construction which ruled in Benloew's day without opposition, and which is accepted to-day also to a very considerable extent, a word is made up of root, suffix, personal inflexion, case-ending, augment, reduplication and so forth, and whichever one of these various elements in the word had been joined to the word last, that was entitled to this higher musical pitch. So *e. g.* in an augment-tense the augment, in a noun in the genitive the genitive ending; when a word was compounded with a preposition, the preposition. As long as this principle was still in existence, the unity of the word in our sense had not as yet developed; the marked emphasis of the 'dernier déterminant' directed the attention of both speaker and hearer so strongly to some part of the whole, to some special element in what afterwards became a unit, that it must be supposed that this accentuation was in force in a period previous to that of word-formation in its strictest sense. The cementing of the word as we have it now was produced by an additional force. By the side of the principle of the last determinant there was developed slowly and gradually a logical principle of accentuation whose purpose it was to act without reference, and in fact in opposition to the specializing tendency of the 'last determinant.' This logical accent, it is assumed, affected the root-syllable, which, in the word as a whole, is the ruling syllable. The further history of accentuation in the separate I. E. languages exhibits, then, a gradual process by which this logical accentuation gains the ascendancy in the word. This in turn is gradually counteracted and affected by the influence of quantity, which Benloew, with true instinct, regards as the last factor which entered the arena. In Sanskrit, as far as is known, the accent is totally independent of any considerations of quantity; in Greek, quantity, especially of the final syllable, begins to exercise an influence on accent; still truer is this of the Latin, where quantity and accent balance each other almost entirely.

The boldness and the *esprit* of Benloew's thoughts on this subject are quite out of proportion with their sobriety, with the extent of the material upon which they were based. In fact they are in all important respects hardly more than ingenious assumptions. Yet his theories deserve even to-day a certain degree of consideration, for they gained such wide adherence that certain of his thoughts are even now silently accepted. So, above all, the musical character of the early I. E. summit-accent, which has never been proved, and which, if separated from stress, is certainly to our ears an extremely peculiar accentuation. Verner, in his explanation of the Old German accent and its influence upon the mute consonants, starts with this statement: 'The I. E. accent was, in its nature, chromatic (*i. e.* musical), and, in its use, of unlimited freedom of position' (KZ. XXIII, p. 128). He then proceeds to explain his exceptions to Grimm's law, by the assumption that the accent became an accent of stress (expiratory) in primitive German, or possibly a combination of musical and stress accent. Benloew's other important idea, namely, that of the 'last determinant,' has also been revived in our day to explain a phenomenon of the widest extent and of great importance, namely, the variation of stem and accentuation in the non-thematic verbal conjugations.[1]

[1] In Greek this variation of stem is preserved intact only in a few cases, and its immediate cause, the shift of accent from the stem to the root, is lost to sight, owing to the leveling force of the recessive accent in verbal accentuation. But the variation of stem-form as well as the accompanying shift of accent is easily established as archaic by comparison with the Vedic Sanskrit, so in the following cases:

εῖ-μι	εἶ(*εἰ-(σ)ι)	εἶ-σι(*εἰ-τι) : ῖ-μεν	ῖ-τε	ῖ-ᾱσι(*ῖ-αντι)
é-mi	é-ṣi	é-ti	: i-mási	i-thás	i-ánti
Foîδ-α	Foîσ-θα	Foîδ-ε	: Fíδ-μεν		
véd-a	vét-tha	véd-a	: vid-má		

The duals, though they agree in both languages in having weak root-form (and accordingly are accented on the personal endings in Sanskrit), are left out

Benloew's work represents the first and also the last attempt on so pretentious a scale to inquire into the original character, development and history of I. E. accentuation. The next somewhat comprehensive work we owe to the founder of comparative philology, Fr. Bopp, in a book entitled 'Vergleichendes Accentuationssystem des Griechischen und des Sanskrit,' Berlin, 1854. This work has really a much narrower scope, it does not profess to deal with general questions in any way, it merely attempts to give an exhaustive list of those words in Greek which have still preserved the accentuation of the Sanskrit and, therefore, in all probability the I. E. accent.

Yet, incidentally, Bopp does express himself on general matters, and in a way that cannot be called happy, either in its method of treating the question or in the result reached. He recognizes as the principle of Sanskrit as well as Greek accentuation 'the greatest possible recession of the tone to the beginning of the word,' p. 16–17. This mode of accentuation possesses the greatest dignity and strength. The limitation of the summit-tone in Greek to the last three syllables he looks upon as a degradation or enervation of

of consideration owing to the problematic character of the endings. In this variation of stem and accent one fact seems clear beyond all doubt, namely, that the weakening of the root is due to the shift of accent to the personal ending; but the question arises, what may be the cause of this varying position of the accent? There has been, as far as is known, but one answer to this question, that of F. De Saussure in his Mémoire sur le Système Primitif des Voyelles dans les Langues Indo-Européennes, p. 189, and that is distinctly in the spirit of Benloew's theory of the 'last determinant.' Saussure assumes with Friedrich Müller (cf. now also Fick in the 'Göttinger Gelehrte Anzeigen' for 1881, Vol. II, part 45, 46, p. 1462) that the so-called secondary personal endings of the verb are more original than the primary, not that the secondary are the result of weakening from the primary, as has been generally held from Bopp's day down. The primary endings often differ from the secondary by an additional _i_, and it is thought that this _i_ is the same deiktic particle which appears, _e. g._ in Greek τουτουί. Thus

	1 _sg._	2 _sg._	3 _sg._	3 _plur._
Primary:	mi	si	ti	nti
Secondary:	m	s	t	nt.

By assuming that the secondary endings first entered into verbal formation and _that these personal endings received the tone, whenever they could_, a reasonable ground is gained for the exceptional position of the three persons of the singular; here the endings are only _m, s, t_, which are not fitted for carrying the tone of the word; therefore the tone remains on the root and preserves in it a stronger vocalization.

language. The accentuation of final syllables or syllables near the
end is due to the 'sinking' of the accent from a position nearer
the beginning of the word, etc. Nowhere, however, does he indicate
in any manner by what process of investigation he came to this
result, though these ideas permeate the entire book and are urged
upon the reader with an evident fondness on the part of the
author. They do not seem to be the result of investigation as to
the nature and quality of the accent of these languages; they are
in fact not offered as such. They are given merely as the *ex
cathedra* opinion of the master who, if any one, has a right to
speak *ex cathedra.*

Since Bopp's book, no comprehensive treatise on I. E. accent
has appeared, nor is it likely that any such pretentious attempt will
be made until investigation in the separate languages has established
a better insight into the special accentuations; there is reason to
hope that the now recognized importance of the study of sentence-
accent will shed much light both upon the original history of accent
in primitive times, as well as upon the ways in which the historical
accentuations of the several languages developed out of the single
Indo-European language.

What we have gained from this discussion of Indo-European
accent is, first, the knowledge that the word-accent was a free one,
restricted to no special syllable or syllables of the word, and
untrammelled by quantity; secondly, that the I. E. language knew
certain well-defined laws of sentence-accentuation, the traces of
which may be fairly looked for in the separate descendants of it.
Thirdly, that the elements which may be supposed to have changed
this original accentuation can scarcely be different from those at
work elsewhere in the formal life of language, regular phonetic
change and analogy. As will be seen, what knowledge we have
of Greek accent calls for no other factor and no other principle, nor
is it likely that any new principle, as yet unknown, will ever exercise any important function in the progress of this difficult study.

III.

We turn now to the Greek itself. The literature of the subject,
both ancient and modern, up to the year 1875 is carefully collected
in the first paragraph of the book of Franz Misteli: ' Über griechische Betonung: Sprachvergleichend-philologische Abhandlungen,'

Paderborn, 1875.[1] Among the ancients the subject is scarcely touched upon in classical times. The first mention of it is in Plato's Cratylus, p. 399, where the terms ὀξύς and βαρύς first turn up; next in order is Aristotle, Poetica, chap. 20, where, in addition to the ὀξύτης and βαρύτης of Plato, a μέσον is mentioned, i. e. a middle-tone, which has been by some exalted to a most important position in the theory of Greek accent, as we shall see soon. Aristarchus in Alexandria is the next authority in chronological order; but above all other works of the ancients, the source for information is Herodian: Herodiani technici reliquiae, collegit, disposuit, emendavit, explicavit, praefatus est Augustus Lentz; especially the first volume containing Lentz's famous preface and the book περὶ καθολικῆς προσῳδίας, to which Misteli gives the first place among his authorities.

In the study of modern writers on this subject one need not go back behind Göttling, Carl Göttling: Allgemeine Lehre vom Accent der griechischen Sprache, Jena, 1835; a book valuable for its digest of the opinions of the Greek grammarians, containing rich collections of material, but of course to-day almost worthless as far as theory and explanation of phenomena are concerned. Next in order are the books of Benloew and Bopp, which have been discussed in the preceding chapter. It may be added that Bopp's book, while almost worthless as far as its general theories

[1] The literature which is given there is more than full enough up to 1875. He omits one book which is practical and valuable for accent of nouns, namely, Chandler, 'A practical introduction to Greek accentuation,' which has appeared lately in a second revised edition, Oxford, 1881. Since Misteli there have appeared in addition to the many and often extremely valuable incidental remarks and minor investigations of comparative grammarians, a few important monographs bearing upon the subject :

Leonhard Masing : Die Hauptformen des Serbisch-Chorwatischen Accents, nebst einleitenden Bemerkungen zur Accentlehre des Griechischen und des Sanskrit, St. Petersburg, 1876, valuable for Greek accent in its first half, pp. 1–49, containing especially an exhaustive criticism of all opinions on the grave accent, §44 fg., p. 19 fg.

Jacob Wackernagel : Der griechische Verbal-accent (KZ. XXIII, p. 457 fg.), of the greatest importance for the general theory of the so-called recessive accent.

Theodor Benfey : Die eigentliche Accentuation des Indicativ Praesentis von ἐς und φά, etc., cited in the note on p. 5. Important for its solution of anastrophe, and its valuable remarks upon enclisis and proclisis.

Leopold von Schroeder : Die Accent-gesetze der homerischen Nominal-composita dargestellt und mit denen des Veda verglichen, KZ. XXIV, 101–28; the first systematic attempt to establish Indo-European laws for the accentuation of compounds.

are concerned, is valuable as a clear and comprehensive exhibition of the facts which it treats, namely, the coincidences in the accentuation of Greek and Sanskrit words. Next, the subject owes some noteworthy and ingenious essays to Franz Misteli and James Hadley; Franz Misteli: Über die Accentuation des Griechischen, KZ. XVII, p. 81 fg., p. 161 fg.; XIX, p. 81 fg.; XXI, p. 16 fg. After the appearance of Hadley's article these essays were rewritten in book-form: Über griechische Betonung: Sprachvergleichend-philologische Abhandlungen, Paderborn, 1875. Hadley's brilliant paper was published no less than three times: On the nature and theory of Greek accent, by James Hadley, from the transactions of the American Philological Association, 1869–70; translated in Curtius Studien, V 407–28, reprinted in Hadley's collected essays, edited by Whitney. Hadley's as well as Misteli's theories, which are closely implicated with one another, will be discussed below. Finally, much important material is contained in the four monographs cited in the foot-note on p. 18.[1]

If we now attempt to give a short general statement with regard to the position of the summit-tone as it appears in Greek, comparing it with that of the free I. E. summit-accent which we have seen established, we may best formulate the facts as follows, under two heads:

1. This free I. E. accentuation has been allowed to continue in Greek in all kinds of formations, *excepting finite forms of the verb*, when the free accent did not go beyond the antepenultima, *e. g.* κλυτός : κλέϜος = ǫrutás : ǫrávas, cf. the Germ. *hlūt* (Ags. *hlūd*); πούς : ποδός = *pā́d* : *padás;* λιπών : ἔλιπον = *ricán* : *áricam, vidván* : *vidúṣi* = εἰδώς (for older *ἰδώς*) : ἰδυῖα, etc. See Bopp, Vgl. Accentuationssystem, pp. 178–84.

2. In all the finite forms of the verb and in all those formations, verbal, nominal, or otherwise, in which the old accentuation stood before the antepenult, a new principle of accentuation has established itself to the exclusion of the old free accent. The chief trait in this new law is that it does not allow the accent to remain on any syllable beyond the antepenult, but restricts it to the last three syllables of the word. To this law there is scarcely an exception in the entire tradition of Greek; the grammarians have fixed the accent of two Aeolic words which contain diaeresis on the syllable

---

[1] Misteli, in his list of authorities, mentions also the most important treatises on Latin and Sanskrit accentuation, which do not, however, concern us so directly.

before the antepenult, Μήδεία in Sappho and the Lesbic ἐπιμέληα, which are not of enough importance for a general discussion. Göttling, p. 20, note 2, and especially Misteli, p. 19, discuss them fully. There are, of course, some words in which the theoretical analysis of forms would lead to seeming exceptions to this law of three syllables, e. g. μέλαινα if we carry it back to its *μέλανια, or θύγατρες if it is derived from *θύγατερες; but this is prehistoric; at the time when the pronunciation was μέλαινα, all reminiscence of an earlier *μέλανια was gone. Within these three last syllables the position of the tone evidently stands in relation to the finer measure of mora, as appears clearly in the law that the accent cannot pass beyond the penultimate when the ultimate is long, so that the Greek accent is, to a considerable extent, restricted to the last three morae, e. g. in such types as ἠδίκουν, διδοῖεν, ἐλέγομεν. To this there is in fact only one seeming exception and one real one:

1. A seeming exception to this restriction to three morae is offered by such cases as e. g. the genitive κήπου, where the acute is apparently four morae from the end of the word, but where in reality the second mora of the long penultima has the tone, so that if we analyze into morae and write *κεέποο, it becomes clear that the exception is only apparent. That the acute on a long vowel means the accentuation of the last mora is not a mere assumption, as is shown by such cases as ἑστώς contracted from ἑσταώς.[1] In such cases a contraction has taken place, and if the tone had been on any other than the last mora the result would have been a circumflex; the reason for the absence of the circumflex is to be found in the fact that the last vowel contains two morae (*ἑστα-όος), with the first of which, the toneless mora, the α contracts; it thus leaves the accent untouched in the result, ἑστώς.[2]

---

[1] That ἑστα-ώς is the old type of this perfect participle can be seen from the Sanskrit equivalent tasthi-vän; here the Sk. i equals the Greek α, as in sthi-tás = στα-τός.

[2] The circumflex cannot display itself upon less than two morae (ʼ ʽ), therefore also this projected *ἑστα-όος results in oxytone ἑστώς. A case where this law of circumflex is clearly exhibited is the vocative of the word Ζεύς. Ζεύς (for *Διεύς) is an old oxytone = Sanskrit dyáús. By an Indo-European law the accent in the vocative recedes to the first syllable of the noun, that is, the tone is as near the beginning of the word as possible. The result for this stem is the vocative Ζεῦ (i. e. Ζέǔ) = dyáüs (i. e. díǎüs). The recession has taken place, but as the word contains but one long vowel, the tone has passed from the last mora to the first, exhibiting at least for diphthongs the actual divisibility of long vowels into morae.

2. The second exception to the law of three morae is much less easily disposed of. When the tone is on the antepenult and the last syllable is therefore short, but the penult is long, then it stands at least on the fourth mora from the end, as *e. g.* in ἄζωστος ; and when both the penult and antepenult are long, apparently on the fifth mora from the end in a case like ἤπειρος.[1] In both of these cases there is, of course, no *a priori* reason why the law of three morae should not have been kept in force by making both words properispomena.[2] The only explanation that the authorities have been able to bring forward is the rather unsatisfactory one which assumes that in such cases the long penultima received a more hurried pronunciation and suffered a loss in quantity. So Göttling, p. 27: 'the penultimate loses a part of its quantitative value because the strength of the tone of antepenult outweighs the following long syllable,' and in the same tone other writers down to Kühner. The difficulty in the way of such an assumption lies, of course, in the metrical value of such toneless long penultimates; they are just as inviolably long as any other long syllables; the ει of ἤπειρος differs in no way metrically from the η of the same word, and the explanation given has quite the appearance of having been constructed *ad hoc* without any sufficient ground. It is not uninteresting that there are quite a number of cases in the language in which both accentuations occur in the same word, one having the tone farther back from the end than the third mora, and the other having it on the third mora. In every case the one which follows the rule of three morae is the older one, *e. g.* ἐρῆμος Epic and in Herodotus, but Attic usually ἔρημος; ὁμοῖος Homeric, Ionic, and Old Attic, later ὅμοιος; τροπαῖον Ionic and Old Attic, common τρόπαιον; in the same way of ἑτοῖμος and ἕτοιμος the first is the more archaic form. In ὁμοῖος : ὅμοιος the historical precedence of ὁμοῖος is easily proven etymologically; ὁμοῖος is a secondary derivative from the oxytone stem ὁμό- = Sk. *samá-* with the secondary suffix -ιο- = Sk. *ya-* (Vedic *-ia*). By an accentual law, which perhaps dates back to the common

---

[1] Apparently only if we assume that the tone is on the last mora of ἤπειρος (*ἐκπειρος) as in κῆπου (*κεέποο).

[2] The extent to which such accentuation is favored in Greek may be best seen in the rendering of such Latin names as *Dentátus, Modéstus, Ahenobárbus,* etc., by Δέντατος, Μόδεστος, Αἰνόβαρβος, etc. Nothing, except the predilection of the language, is in the way of such an accentuation as Δευτάτος, etc. Hadley in Curtius's Studien, V, p. 413.

Indo-European period,[1] such a combination as ὁμό + ιο yields ὁμοῖο-, *i. e.* ὁμδίο-, cf. the case of Ζεῦ (*i. e.* Ζεύ) discussed above on p. 20, note. We might then see in such cases the trace of a still more stringent law in favor of the three morae; possibly the principle which underlies the recessive accent started strictly from that point.

Whatever this law of three morae is, it may be noticed right here that it is also the Greek law for enclisis, *i. e.* a Greek word can incline upon the preceding word only in such a way that the result does not produce conditions which are in conflict with the law of three morae as laid down above. So *e. g.* Ζεύς μοι offers the conditions which are apparent in κῆπου; καλός ἐστι,[2] the same conditions as ἄζωστος. When, however, it is desired to incline ἡμῶν, ἡμῖν, ἡμᾶς, or ὑμῶν, ὑμῖν, ὑμᾶς, the result is Ζεὺς ἥμων, Ζεὺς ἥμιν or ἥμιν (with a shortening of the last vowel which may stand in connection with the removal of the tone from the ultima), etc. That is to say, owing to the fact that these words contain at least four morae they cannot become entirely enclitic, but become so as much as possible. The grammars[3] (*e. g.* Hadley, §232) do not understand this phenomenon, when they describe ἥμων, etc., merely as optional weaker forms, and not as enclitic forms.[4] Aside from the testimony in favor of

---

[1] The circumflex in such cases is probably Indo-European, for in Sanskrit also the acute vowel on the *a* of *samá-* would be followed by the so-called enclitic *svarita* on the next syllable (*ia*), which seems to imply that the voice instead of sinking from the acute to lowest pitch without mediation, passes down gradually, and this amounts evidently to the same phonetic result as the circumflex in ὁμοῖο-. See Whitney in the Proceedings of the American Philological Association, 1870, p. 9; Sk. Gramm. §85.

[2] The grammars falsely set up the paradigm εἰμί, ἐστί, ἐσμέν, etc. The words are enclitics and receive this acute only when enclisis of the entire word is made impossible because the result would leave too many morae unaccented. The accent is therefore due to sentence-law and is not etymological. The true accent of ἐστι is preserved in orthotone ἔστι, see below, p. 41. The reason why these words as well as φημί, etc., are enclitic will be discussed in full below, p. 37.

[3] Kühner calls it 'eine ganz eigenthümliche Art der Deklination,' I, p. 264.

[4] The assumption of enclisis in the shorter forms (μοι, μου), but of orthotonesis or a merely changed accent in the longer forms (ἥμιν, ἥμας), apparently receives a certain kind of support from the Sanskrit, where the enclisis of the personal pronouns of the first and second persons, being evidently of a piece with the enclisis of the same persons in Greek, is also restricted to *monosyllabic* forms. The pronouns of the third person, *i. e.* the various demonstrative stems which perform that function, do, however, incline forms of more than one syllable freely, *e. g. asmai* 'to him,' *asya* 'of him,' are used both orthotonically and

enclisis that is afforded by the parallelism of, *e. g.* μοι and μου, when compared with ἐμοί and ἐμοῦ, we have most interesting native authority to the effect that in Greek pronouns, the recession of the accent in accordance with the law of three morae was the substitute of enclisis when the word inclined possessed itself at least four morae. Wackernagel, in KZ. XXIII 458, cites from Apollon. Synt. p. 130, a passage, also treated by Lehrs, Quaestiones epicae, p. 123, which bears upon this question : ἠρκέσθη ἡ ἔγκλισις διὰ τῆς μεταθέσεως τοῦ τόνου, ἥκουσ᾽ ἥμων . . . τῆς τάσεως μετατιθεμένης κατὰ τὴν ἄρχουσαν· ἠδυνάτει γὰρ ἐπὶ τὸ προκείμενον προσελθεῖν. This passage, from excellent ancient authority, proves almost beyond a doubt what seems in every other way also probable, namely, that ἥμων, ὕμων, etc., are cases of enclisis, and that, therefore, enclisis and recessive accent are ruled by the same law of three morae. The same principle is, of course, patent in other well-known attempts to observe the same law ; in fact if we take the cases which Hadley gives in §107 : ἄνθρωπός τις, παιδές τινές, λόγοι τινές, we have in every case an enclisis which is rectified or rather cut short by the law of three morae, as exhibited in the general recessive accent ; it is to be noted that the position of the tone on the fourth mora from the end is also exhibited here, when the penult has a long vowel and the ultima is short, οὔ φησι like ἤπειρος, λόγοι τι(νές) like ἄζωστος. It will be seen below, p. 36, of what importance it has been thought, that the laws which govern the scope of enclisis, and of recession of the Greek accent, are identical. Wackernagel's theory about the recessive accent, which has commended itself to the acceptance of most modern grammarians, is in the main based upon this coincidence.

IV.

If, in stating the most prominent views with regard to the peculiar character of Greek accentuation, we were to begin with Göttling, this would be done in deference to a book which must still be kept at one's elbow in the study of this subject. In some respects it might

enclitically, cf. above, p. 11, note 2. It may be further said that the Sanskrit proves nothing against the enclitic character of such forms as ἥμων by the side of ἡμῶν, because it happens to possess different polysyllabic forms made from different stems by the side of the monosyllabic ones. It is not surprising that a language which can choose between *asmábhyam* and *nas* for the dative plural of the personal pronoun of the first person, should choose *asmábhyam* when it required an orthotone form, but *nas* when it desired enclisis. The Greek has no such choice in the cases involved.

still be necessary to warn against it, while in others it might be mentioned profitably as a scientific *curiosum* of efforts in this direction, not as yet fifty years old. Göttling might also perhaps deserve a mention because he represents the last attempt to account for Greek accentuation, entirely out of itself, though even he occasionally takes a glance at the incipient work of comparative philology—he often refers to Humboldt and Bopp—or brings on some real or seeming parallelism from some other language. Occasionally again he sees farther than some of his successors, as when he recognizes the fact that the recessive accentuation began in the non-Aeolic dialects with the finite verb. The neglect of this fact is one of the weakest spots in the theory of Misteli-Hadley, which will be discussed immediately. Yet the limited space of an article forbids any systematic mention of Göttling's views, and as the views of Benloew and Bopp are already disposed of, we can at once turn to the Misteli-Hadley theory. Misteli's theory on the peculiar form of Greek accentuation was based upon comparative studies as well as 'philological' investigations in the Greek grammarians. It was first laid down in Vols. XVII, XIX and XXI of Kuhn's Zeitschrift, and afterwards embodied in the form of a book, whose title was given above, p. 17. In the period between Misteli's articles and Misteli's book there appeared Hadley's article in the Proceedings of the American Philological Association (cited *ibid.*), an article which aimed to rectify Misteli's theory, and which extended it by bringing in the Latin within the framework of the theory. Therefore the name Misteli-Hadley theory.

The key to the explanation of the three-syllable or three-morae accent according to this theory is the assumption of a middle-tone (mittel-ton) which, already in the parent-language, followed immediately upon every summit-tone, as a kind of intermediate step which served to bring the voice gradually from the musical height of the summit to the lowest depth (the toneless syllable). Nowhere was the passage from the summit-tone to tonelessness in the same word one which did not involve this middle-tone. If there were syllables left in the word after the two which are bespoken for the summit-tone and the middle-tone, these—and their number is left indefinite—are toneless, or according to the preferable terminology of the German receive the 'tief-ton.' This theory of a middle-tone is suggested in the first place by the Vedic Sanskrit. This possesses a mode of accentuation which distinguishes three kinds of tone, 1. a higher (*udātta* 'raised') or acute; 2. a lower (*anuddātta* 'not raised '), *i. e.* toneless or 'tief-tonig'; 3. a third, which is called *svarita*, according to Whitney §81 is always of secondary origin, being the result of actual combination of an acute vowel and a following toneless vowel into one syllable. This is uniformly defined by the natives as compound in pitch, a union of higher and lower tone within the limits of a single syllable. It is thus identical, as far as can be seen, with the Greek and Latin circumflex, and in all probability goes back with the circumflex to the common I. E. period, as *e. g.* in the case voc. Ζεῦ : *dyāùs* = nom. Ζεύς : *dyāús*, discussed on p. 20, note 2.

So far everything is in reasonable accord with Greek notions of accent. But there is a further element. 'The Hindu grammarians agree in declaring the (naturally toneless) syllable following an acute, whether in the same or in another word, to be *svarita* or circumflex, unless indeed it be itself followed by an acute or circumflex, in which case it retains its grave tone. This is called by European scholars the enclitic or dependent circumflex,' Whitney, §85. Misteli and Hadley then impugn the statement of the native grammarians that this was a circumflex, and regard it as incomparably more probable that this *svarita* is a middle-tone. And Whitney, who is the first authority in matters of native Vedic grammar, says (§85) 'This seems to mean that the voice, which is borne up at the higher pitch to the end of the acute syllable, does not ordinarily drop to grave pitch by an instantaneous movement, but descends by a more or less perceptible slide in the course of the following syllable. No Hindu authority suggests the theory of a middle or intermediate tone for the enclitic, any more than for the independent circumflex. For the most part, the two are identified with one another in treatment and designation.' Whitney's opinion with regard to the enclitic *svarita*, while it denies it the name of middle-tone, does, we can see, nevertheless support a kind of tone which does not lie very far removed in its nature from that middle-tone in favor of which Misteli and Hadley argue.

But on the other hand the testimony for a middle-tone in Greek which attaches itself immediately to the summit-tone in the manner of the enclitic *svarita* is extremely weak, in fact may be said not to exist at all. Not that there is not mention made by the ancients of other accents than the three familiar ones. Aristotle, Poetica, ch. 20, and Rhet. 3, 1, 4 mentions a μέσον in addition to the ὀξύτης and βαρύτης of Plato, and this, according to Misteli, p. 44, note, and Hadley, Cu. Stud. V 417, is probably a middle-tone, though both

admit the possibility that the circumflex is indicated by it. The
Greek grammarian, Tyrannio from Amisus, who was captured by
Lucullus and brought to Rome, reports four accents according to
Varro (in Servius de accentibus, cf. A. Wilmans de M. Terenti
Varronis libris grammaticis, p. 187). Varro mentions other Greek
grammarians who report more than three accents; there are in fact
those who report six accents altogether. Misteli seeks further (§7,
p. 50) to fasten this middle-accent immediately after the summit-
tone, in a manner parallel with the enclitic *svarita*, by the aid of a
well-known passage of Dionysius of Halicarnassus de comp. verbo-
rum liber, section XI, but in this attempt he positively fails. The
passage reads διαλέκτου μὲν οὖν μέλος ἑνὶ μετρεῖται διαστήματι τῷ λεγομένῳ
διὰ πέντε, *i. e.* the two limits of tone in spoken speech (between
summit-tone and low-tone) are said to be a fifth. Now Misteli
argues that this interval must have been mediated by the middle-
tone in passing from an accented syllable to an unaccented one,
because the unmediated skip of the voice through a fifth would
give to the language 'einen schneidenden und widerwärtigen
character,' and because Greek 'speech would move in extremes' in
such a case. But as Masing, *loc. cit.* p. 23, points out, another
passage in the same author makes this construction impossible.
For Dionysius continues, not many lines beyond this passage, with
the antithesis to the μέλος διαλέκτου in the following manner: ἡ δὲ
ὀργανικὴ τε καὶ ᾠδικὴ μοῦσα διαστήμασί τε χρῆται πλείοσιν, οὐ διὰ πέντε μόνον,
ἀλλ' ἀπὸ τοῦ διὰ πασῶν ἀρξαμένη, καὶ τὸ διὰ πέντε μελῳδεῖ, καὶ τὸ διὰ τεσσά-
ρων, κ. τ. λ. 'Music, however, instrumental as well as vocal, employs
several intervals; not only fifths, but, to begin with octaves, next
fifths, fourths, etc.' It is evident from this passage that Dionysius
recognizes a plurality of intervals only for music and not for common
speech, and it appears that according to this author there is but
one interval, the fifth, in use in speech.

Moreover, this passage by no means certainly describes word-
accent; so *e. g.* Göttling, who by the way denies that Greek word-
accent was musical at all, construes this διαλέκτου μέλος as a rhetorical sentence-accent. Certainly it cannot be brought in as testimony
in favor of that special kind of middle-tone which follows every
summit-accent. Hadley does indeed recognize that the testimony
of the ancients for it, or for that matter any middle-tone, leaves
much to be desired; but argues that the peculiar effectiveness of
it in the theory which he defends and extends is the surer testimony
in favor of its actual existence.

The theory is then completed by the following assumption, which is to account for both Greek and Latin accentuation: *There was developed in the Graeco-Italic division of the family, after they had separated from the common stock, a disinclination to allow more than one toneless syllable to follow upon the middle-tone;* this disinclination caused a moving forward of the summit-accent to such a position that there was room after it, and after the middle-tone which necessarily followed it, for only one toneless syllable. Thus originated the Graeco-Italic law by which the summit-accent is restricted to one of the last three syllables of a word. The immediate ancestors of the Greeks and Romans, the ' Graeco-Italians,' before their separation from one another, accented their words alike according to this simple law, *e. g.* *ἐλείπομην*, *ἄνθρωπου*, *gaudērēs*, *légendus, i. e.* all words which originally had the summit-tone *before* the antepenult simply shifted it to the antepenult, thus producing a very special cadence agreeable to the Graeco-Italic ear, *summit-tone, middle-tone, tonelessness* (low tone). In words which did not have the tone anterior to the antepenult, words like λελυμένος, χαλεπός, the accent remained undisturbed; for here there was no room for the violation of the law that the middle-tone should not be followed by more than one toneless syllable. But as Greeks and Italians divided off they developed their common three-syllable tone-law in a manner which led to pretty sharp differences. The point of departure from the Graeco-Italic law was the *toneless* syllable in the cadence for the Greeks, the *middle-tone* for the Italians.

Let us first remain a while with the Greeks. They developed a dislike for a *long* toneless, *i. e.* final, syllable, so that the Graeco-Italic cadence of summit-tone, middle-tone, toneless syllable, was modified for the Greek into summit-tone, middle-tone, and *short* toneless syllable, whenever the accent had originally, in I. E. times, stood before the antepenult. In order to exhibit the application of this law, Hadley divides the phenomena of the Greek recessive accent into four divisions, and one need but remember in addition that he regards the circumflex as a compound accent containing both summit and middle-tone, in order to understand his reasoning.

1. The simplest case. The acute cannot stand on any syllable before the antepenult, therefore I. E. *ἐλείπετο* becomes Greek ἐλείπετο.

2. The antepenult must, if it takes the accent, take the acute; *ἐλείπετο (i. e. *ἐλίπετο*) is impossible, because it leaves two toneless syllables at the end.

3. When the penultimate carries the accent and the ultimate contains a long vowel, then this must be the acute, τοιαύτη, not τοιαύτη (= *τοιαύτη), because this would result in a *long* toneless syllable.

4. A long vowel in the penultimate must take the circumflex if the ultimate is short, τοιοῦτος, not *τοιοῦτος, because there would be no room for the toneless syllable.[1]

This method of accentuation in the separate life of the Greek also did not gain ground when it was necessary to draw the summit-tone back from the end in order to gain the desired cadence. Therefore types like λελυμένος, λιπών, remained undisturbed.[2]

Only one division of the Greek people, the Aeolians of Asia Minor, took also this step completely, that is they subjected their entire accentuation to the law of cadence, summit-tone, middle-tone, low tone, therefore λελύμενος, χαλέπως. Where the entire cadence was not to be procured, as in σοφός, they drew the accent back at least as far as possible, σόφος.

The theory then proceeds to explain the Latin accent by assuming that the Graeco-Italic cadence-accentuation there also received a modification, namely, that there developed with the Italians a disinclination against a long middle-tone, so that the Latin cadence became summit-tone, short middle-tone, low tone. We will return to the Latin further on and see that this theory accounts for the Latin system about as well as for the Greek. At present the Greek will be dealt with alone.

1. In the first place it has been shown that the assumption of this middle-tone following every summit-tone is a purely theoretic one, and that the testimony of the grammarians in favor of such a middle-tone amounts to nothing at all. Not that it is to be supposed that the Greek word did not possess subsidiary tones just as much as words of to-day; but the assumption of a special middle-tone which must follow the summit, implying that the pitch of the summit was especially high, so as to stand in need of a mediator between it and the low tone, is warranted by no fact of Greek grammar or

---

[1] This is the weak spot in the arrangement. The theory by which the explanation of the Greek accent is here attempted does not in reality claim that the cadence, *summit-tone, middle-tone, low tone*, must be established in every case; it makes only the negative claim that after summit-tone and middle-tone *no more than one* low tone should follow. This condition would be satisfied as well by *τοιοῦτος as by τοιοῦτος.

[2] This rule knows exceptions from the earliest times. So *e. g.* nouns in -τις (-σις), ῥύσις, τίσις, are originally oxytone formations, Sk. *srutis, citis,* and yet appear in all periods of the language with recessive accent, cf. below, p. 30.

tradition. The passage of Dionysius not only proves nothing, but if it speaks of word-accent at all, disproves the existence of any interval in the διαλέκτου μέλος, except the fifth.

2. The assumption of a Graeco-Italian accentuation (ἐλείπομην, *légendus*) stands entirely in the air. Not one historical fact is in its favor; it is solely based upon the fact of the restriction of the accent to the last three syllables. At the time when Misteli and Hadley wrote, the assumption of a Graeco-Italic period was very generally, though even then not universally, accepted. It is to-day a theory of the past. In just that particular factor of form which stands in especially close relation to accent, namely, vocalism, these families are about as far removed from one another as possible. Further, it will be urged below that the Greek recessive, or, to speak with Hadley, cadence-accent, began with the *verb;* it is precisely in the verb that Greek and Latin have diverged so extensively that mere fragments of the older system of formations are left in the latter, and it is altogether improbable that the Latin should have saved an old system of verbal accentuation for a new and obscure set of formations.

3. The assumption of the sequence, summit-tone, middle-tone, and short toneless syllable, is after all nothing more than the formulation into a more complicated shape of the simple law that the recessive accent does not recede beyond three, or in one case (forms like ἄζωστος and ἤπειρος) four morae. The theory does not find it possible to free itself from the count by mora any more than the formulation by which the accent was described above. While it appears to dispose of the case of ἄζωστος better (for here it was necessary above to assume recession to four morae), it is deficient in cases like τοιοῦτος, because it does not account for the constant circumflex, cf. p. 28, note 1, which on the other hand is accounted for perfectly within the theory of the three morae.

4. Finally, the last objection is one which more than any other undermines the middle-tone theory. The original I. E. succession of summit-tone, middle-tone, low tone, it is claimed was in Graeco-Italian times moved down a place or two or even more in order to pander to a dislike on the part of the Graeco-Italians to allow more than one toneless syllable after the middle-tone. An aesthetic dislike which is powerful enough to reform the accent of an entire language in a thoughtful, laborious manner, is a sufficiently doubtful factor in modern linguistic explanation. It cannot exactly be called a phonetic law, because a phonetic law acts spontaneously, and

would not be likely to count the syllables of a certain word, and then, upon finding that the summit-tone upon a certain syllable would leave too many toneless syllables at the end, move it down a sufficient number of morae to ward off such an event. At least so complicated a process must seem highly improbable when it is compared with the workings of such a law in other quarters. Yet the explanation as a phonetic law might, for lack of a better one, be accepted with reserve, but for the fact that the theory fails to account for a strictly grammatical, and not aesthetic, fact connected with it; namely this, that the recessive accent has most certainly in Greek begun with the finite verb, *where there is practically no exception to it;* that it excludes, with particular care, non-finite forms of the verb in the same tense-system and in evident connection with finite forms, exhibiting thus on Greek ground a most outspoken character as a grammatical quality of finite verbs: ἔλιπον, ἐλιπόμην, λίπω, etc., but λιπών, λιπεῖν, λιπέσθαι, etc. Of course noun-formations are not spared in historical times. But here the tendency is not regulated by any traceable law. Certain noun-categories become recessive; others, with apparently the same claim to favor, do not; so adjectives in -ύς *versus* nouns in -τις (σις).[1] It is in fact perfectly clear that the recessive accent in Greek, whatever its explanation, started with the finite forms of the verb, and thence succeeded in attacking nominal formations also; it cannot, therefore, have been due to the disinclination of the Graeco-Italians to allow two toneless syllables after the middle-tone. Such a cause cannot have differentiated between noun and verb.

V.

The strength of Misteli's system as completed by Hadley seems at first sight to lie in the fact that it includes the Latin, which shares with the Greek the sufficiently remarkable quality of restricting the summit-tone to the last three syllables of a word. This coincidence Hadley explains by the assumption of a Graeco-Italic accent which knew no restriction except this, that the assumed I. E. cadence of summit-tone, middle-tone and low tone, when it began before

---

[1] Both are originally oxytone noun-formations; the adjectives in -ύς have remained so, θρασύς = Sk. *dhṛṣús*, βραδύς = Sk. *mṛdús*, πλατύς = Sk. *pṛthús*, ἐλαχύς = Sk. *raghús*, παχύς = Sk. *bahús*, βαρύς = Sk. *gurús*, etc.; the nouns in -τις have without exception become recessive, as in the cases of ῥύσις and τίσις, cited above, p. 28, note 2.

the antepenult, was moved down to avoid more than one low tone
at the end of the word. After the separation of the Greeks from
the Italians, the two peoples refined the common Graeco-Italic
accent; the Greek by insisting upon summit-tone, middle-tone,
short low tone, the Lat. by developing a fondness for summit-tone,
short middle-tone, and indifferent low-tone. Accordingly the
Graeco-Italic accentuation, which still permitted forms like *légendus, gaudērēs*, etc., was modified; and this modification again
becomes at least superficially easy if the definition and description
of the Latin circumflex, as given by the Latin grammarians, is
remembered, cf. Corssen, Ueber Aussprache, Vocalismus und Betonung der lateinischen Sprache, II, p. 800 fg. According to them
the Lat. circumflex was employed upon long monosyllables (excepting *nē* with the imperative), and on penultimas with long vowels
(not, however, by position) when the ultimate was short. Everywhere else the acute was employed according to the remaining
well-known rules. How much value is to be attached to the statement that in Latin *gaudēre* had the circumflex, made as that statement is by grammarians who were under the influence of Greek
grammar down to the minutest particulars, is after all an open
question; even Curtius, a strong supporter of the Graeco-Italic
accentuation, has said in my hearing that "der Circumflex im
lateinischen bedeutet überhaupt nicht viel, ist mehr auf Theorie
gegründet." [1]

But the assumption of the existence of the circumflex, and the
cadence projected for the Latin, summit-tone, *short* middle-tone,
and low-tone, seemingly procure a satisfactory arrangement of the
historical phenomena.

The simplest case is that of types like *légérĕ* and *légĕrĕt;* here
the cadence, summit-tone, short middle-tone, and low-tone, is easily
procured. In the type *gaudēre*, the same result is procured by
dividing the circumflexed *ē* between summit-tone and middle-tone,
quasi *gaudĕērĕ*. Greater is the difficulty in the type *gaudērēs*,
for the first *ē* is not circumflexed, therefore the syllable *rēs* must
furnish the place for both middle-tone and low-tone, *gaudērēĕs;*
but who will after all believe that there was so thoroughgoing a

---

[1] Petrus Lange is the strongest assailant of the Latin circumflex, in three
treatises: De grammaticorum latinorum praeceptis quae ad accentum spectant,
Bonn, 1857; in a critique of Weil and Benloew's Théorie générale de l'accentuation latine, in Fleckeisen's Jahrbücher, Vol. 79, 1859, p. 44–71; Untersuch-
ungen über den lateinischen Accent, in Philologus 31, p. 98–121.

difference in the accentuation of the two words *gaudēri* and *gaudēres*, or upon what tangible fact in the life of the language is this differentiation based ? And in the type *legéndŭs* we are left without a place for the low-tone, because *gen* cannot take the circumflex, *legéndŭs*, while the type *legéndi* again divides its final long syllable between middle and low-tone, *legéndĭ̄*. Here the arrangement is weakest ; it institutes a complicated difference between the accent of *gaudēri* (*gaudēēri*) and *legéndŭs* (*legéndŭs* ≅), which is devoid of all foundation in the actual and not hypothetical life and history of the language.

Of the four main objections which were urged above against this theory when applied to the Greek, three hold good against Latin also ; others can be added from the point of view of the Latin itself.

1. The still more complete absence of testimony in favor of a middle-tone which regularly followed the summit-tone. There is no such testimony at all to be obtained from the Latin.

2. The assumption of the Graeco-Italic accent, against which what was said above, p. 29, is to be compared.

3. The combination with Greek recessive accent, which has originated with the verb, and will be shown below to be due to an I. E. law pertaining to the verb, which therefore separates that method of accentuation incontrovertibly from the Latin, where the special influence of the verb is not to be thought of, and has not, as far as is known, ever been suggested.

4. The very similarity of the Latin accent to the Greek becomes, if we look more narrowly, reduced to the restriction of the tone to the last three syllables. In every other respect the accentuations of the two languages stand in the sharpest opposition to one another.

a. In Greek the summit-tone is not excluded from the last syllable, in Latin it is so entirely.

b. In Greek the penult is absolutely without influence as far as deciding the position of the summit-tone is concerned ; in Latin the penult is the pivot around which everything revolves, its quantity decides the position of the accent.

c. Just as indifferent as the penult is in Greek, so in Latin the ultima has no influence upon the position of the accent, while in Greek it is the main factor in determining the position of the recessive accent.

5. A fifth reason against the assumption of the Graeco-Italic accent is presented by the fact that there are distinct traces in Latin of an accentuation which was not restricted to the last three syllables.

The law of three syllables was preceded in an archaic period by a freer accentuation, the vestiges of which are not sufficiently numerous to make it possible to describe its exact character, though enough can be seen to render it probable that it did not know this restriction, at least not in the form of an inviolable law.

a. Very strong indications of a different régime in matters of accentuation are contained in the vowel changes which attend reduplication and composition. The reduplication and prepositional prefixes in Latin exercise an influence upon the vocalism of Latin roots which would remain unexplained, unless it be assumed that they once regularly received the accent. Thus, when *júro* becomes in composition *pé-jéro, facio* becomes **cón-ficio, gnōtus* (with very old vocalism = Greek γνωτός = Sk. *jñātás*) becomes *có-gnĭtus ;* it is necessary to assume that the accent stood originally upon the preposition at a time when the root-vowel was not as yet weakened (**pé-júro, *có-gnōtus*), and therefore accented in a manner thoroughly different from the laws of accent in historical times ; for it would be incredible that this weakening of the root-vowel should take place under the summit-tone (**pé-júro,* etc). This accentuation of the **preposition** with the finite forms of the verb inclining upon them is Indo-European, and at any rate an accentual condition which must be admitted for the Latin at some remote period. On the same principle *con-fício* must have originated from a prehistoric **cón-facio,* with the accent on a syllable anterior to the antepenult. And, further, in the perfects, *tetigi, pepigi, cecini,* **fefelli, cecĭdi** (: *cado*), *cecīdi* (: *caedo*), the weakening of the root-vowels is due to the accentuation of the reduplicating syllable ; this leads to forms like **tétigimus,* etc., which again have the tone before the **antepenult.** Moreover, certain Italian forms not Latin support this view. *E. g.* the Oscan forms *fe-fāc-id* (perfect optative third singular), or *fe-fāc-ust* (future perfect third singular), when compared with Latin *con-fic-io,* or with an ideal reduplicated **fé-fic-i* from **fé-fāc-i,* show that this regular weakening of the root-syllables is a special Latin phenomenon ; so also Umbrian *Jupater* is probably the common Italian predecessor of Latin *Jupiter.* If this weakening of the vowels, as would appear from such examples, is not common to all Italian dialects, but belongs especially to the Latin branch, and if it is assumed correctly that these weakenings would be impossible under an accent like *fefācust, fefácid,* we have an historical corroboration in actually occurring Italian words of the assumption that the three-syllable accent is a special Latin feature, not common even to all the Italian dialects; this disproves a Graeco-Italic accentuation directly on Italian ground, aside from the general considerations which have been brought on above. It must be assumed, then, that *fé-fác-id* was the old accentuation; this accent weakened the root-syllable *fāc* in Latin alone, and after that pattern the same process is assumed necessarily for forms of more than three syllables, *cónficio, díspliceo, displicemus, displicebamus*, etc.[1]

b. Other isolated forms, not within verbal paradigms, lend also a certain support to the assumption of a freer position of the Latin accent previous to the purely quantitative one of historical times. Thus, when early *opitumo-* becomes later *optumo-*, it seems very improbable that the *i* should have been lost under the accent; an original accentuation, **ópitumo-* seems much more probable. *Samnium* is for **Sabinium*, (cf. Oscan *Safínim*); the accent of this **Sabinium* seems again to have stood on the first syllable, this alone accounts satisfactorily for the loss of the *i*. Again, when the Greek Πολυδεύκης passes through *Polouces, Pollūces*, into *Pollux*, it seems also improbable that these weakenings at the end should have taken place under the accent *Poludeúces*, though in a proper name it is not certain but what popular etymology may have contributed to the corruption. Other forms favorable to this older accentuation are cited by Corssen, Aussprache, Vocalismus, Betonung, etc., II[1], 902 fg.; Kritische Beitraege, 577 fg.

c. Less important is the statement of the grammarian Nigidius Figulus, as reported by Gellius, that proper names in *io* in the vocative accent the first syllable, *e. g. Váleri*, fr. *Valerius*. Gellius

---

[1] A great part of this argument against the assumed Graeco-Italian three-syllable law was made as early as Kuhn's Zeitschrift, Vol. IX, p. 77, by Lottner. Curtius, in an article in the same volume, p. 321 fg., attempts to refute Lottner's assumption that forms like *conficio* prove an accent before the antepenult (**cónficio*), by assuming that this weakening process started in forms which contained but three syllables, *e. g. cón-facit, cónficit*, and was thence generalized for the entire paradigm; accordingly the paradigm of this tense was originally **confácio, cónficis, cónficit, *confácimus, *confácitis, *confáciunt*, and only later the long forms assumed secondarily the vowel of the short ones, *conficimus*, etc. This explanation is insufficient, first, because there is no trace of any such forms as **confacio* to be found anywhere in Latin; secondly, because it is impossible to assign any reason why the numerically stronger forms like **confácio* should have always succumbed to those with the weaker vowels, and why the reverse process did not occasionally take place. There is too much consistency and regularity in the use of the weak vowels to render such an explanation at all probable.

himself, it appears, remarks that such a pronunciation would have been laughed at in his day, and Nigidius Figulus was also in other respects a peculiar scholar, who set up a special terminology and indulged in other idiosyncrasies for accentual words. The possibility that he merely theorizes on Greek vocative patterns is not to be denied. But Benfey, Der indo-germanische Vocativ, p. 51, enthusiastically defends his view, saying that even if in Gellius's time such a pronunciation was laughable, it may nevertheless be a learned possession of Nigidius, a quasi 'lectio doctissima,' and employs it to establish by its aid the Indo-European accentual law, otherwise also secure enough, namely, that vocatives were accented on the first syllable, regardless of the accent of their themes under other circumstances.

Against all this stands then the single fact of the restriction within three syllables, a fact striking enough on the outside, but yet not very significant if we remember certain other facts. The possibility that two I. E. languages, starting from the common stock and from a common point of departure, should leave that point behind them, work out their accentual destiny separately and very differently, and should yet arrive in the end at a certain similarity in historical times, can be proved in more striking cases than that of Greek and Latin. Polish, we saw above, regularly accents the penult; the same thing is true of the Cymric (Welsh); while their respective closest sisters, the Bohemian and the Irish, accent the first syllable. No one would therefore presume to hint at any kinship either between Polish and Cymric, or between Bohemian and Irish, closer than that warranted by the general fact that they all belong to the I. E. family. On the other hand the Lithuanian and Lettish both belong to the Lithuanian branch of the Lithu-Slavic family, and they are so closely related to one another in sound and form that Lithuanian may be changed into Lettish by the observance of a moderate number of phonetic laws; yet they have gone so far apart in their accentuations that the Lithuanian still preserves, to a fair extent, the free I. E. accentuation, while the Lettish regularly accents the first syllables of all words. And it may not be improper to point out that the Arabic shows a striking resemblance in its laws of accent with the Latin, as may be seen in Caspari's Arabic Grammar, fourth edition, Halle, 1876, p. 22. It will appear that Arabic accentuation is identical with Latin, (1) in never accenting the last syllable of words of more than one syllable; (2) in always accenting a long penult; (3) in never accenting a short penult. In fact it possesses every law of the Latin excepting its restriction of the tone within the last three syllables. Who would on that account alone attempt to establish kinship between the accentual methods of the two languages? Therefore the supposed common origin of the Greek and Latin systems of accentuation stands upon the weakest possible ground, and an explanation of the Greek recessive accent which ignores the external similarity of the Latin may now be approached with reasonable confidence.

VI.

The explanation of the Greek recessive accent must start from *the finite forms of the verb*, where alone it is evidently at home. This special nexus between the verb and the accent is not noticed by Misteli and Hadley, and has been pointed out above as the weakest point in their system. Yet the fact had been noticed and utilized to a certain extent even by Göttling, who puts the verb on the same level with the Aeolic accent in this respect. It is Wackernagel's merit and the reason of his success that he began his investigation with this fact as the basis. And he has succeeded, as will be now shown, in explaining the Greek accent, as far as the verb is concerned, by a series of qualities or laws of treatment to which the finite verb was subjected in *sentence-nexus* in I. E. times, so that the Greek recessive accent appears to be a development of tone-laws pertaining to *sentence*-accent in distinction from *word*-accent. We must from the start let the etymological accent of the individual word lie latent, or better, keep in mind that the etymological accent of a word may under certain circumstances vanish under the influence of sentence-accentuation.

Wackernagel starts with the observation that both in Greek and in Sanskrit the finite verb is occasionally subjected to enclisis, of course with the greatest possible differences in other respects. In Sanskrit, every finite verb becomes enclitic under certain conditions and according to certain laws (see Whitney, Sk. Gramm. §592 fg.). In Greek only two verbs in the present indicative, εἰμι and φημι, are enclitic. The old explanation, according to which this enclisis was due to paleness of meaning, he rejects justly, because φημι is no paler than λέγω.[1] He assumes, then, that this restriction of the

---

[1] So far is this from being true that ΦΗΜΙ is, and continues to be, the strongest of the verbs of saying, often meaning 'aver,' 'asseverate,' and sometimes actually taking μή as if a verb of swearing. λέγω in Homer is not yet a full verb of saying.—B. L. G.

enclisis to these two indicatives is due to the Greek law of enclisis, according to which an enclitic word may not contain more than two syllables and three morae. This, it will be remembered, was exhibited in detail above, p. 22, where the examples Ζεύς ἥμιν, etc., with enclisis of the orthotone ἡμῖν, was shown to be the substitute of the enclisis which is exhibited in Ζεύς μοι. Of course these are not the only individual Greek finite verbal forms which, in spite of this restriction to three morae, could be inclined, but here Wackernagel recognizes with consummate acuteness that the present indicatives of these roots represent the only cases in the language where the entire paradigm of the tense or mood would allow the enclisis throughout. A form like λέγω, πεῖθε, ἦσαν would by itself be capable of enclisis, but not λέγομεν, λέγετε, πείθετε, ἦστην; therefore enclisis could not sustain itself in the paradigms to which these words belong; on the other hand, the *undisturbed* capacity for enclisis of εἰμι, (εἰ), εστι, εστον, εσμεν, εστε, εισι; φημι, (φής),[1] φησι, φατον, φαμεν, φατε, φασι, without a single interloper that would be debarred from enclisis by containing too many morae, is the secret of the preservation of their enclisis. The test for other tense or modesystems is easily made and will always bring up some form containing either more than two syllables or three morae. The enclisis of these two present indicatives is then identical with the enclisis in Ζεύς μοι.

The question now arises: What has happened to the other verbs which were debarred from enclisis by containing too many morae? Precisely the same treatment that has happened to an enclitic pronoun of too many morae. They were inclined as much as possible, in accordance with the principle exhibited in the change of orthotone ἡμῖν to enclitic ἥμιν, and orthotone ἡμῶν to enclitic ἥμων; just as Ζεύς ἥμων contains orthotone ἡμῶν changed to ἥμιν, just so does Ζεύς δοίη contain the prehistoric δοιή = Sk. *deyāt;* however, not in its orthotone, but in its enclitic form, for δοίη is the enclitic to *δοιή just as much as ἥμων is the enclitic of ἡμῶν. This may be formulated in the following proportion:

$$\text{Ζεύς μοι : Ζεύς ἥμων = Ζεύς ἐστι : Ζεύς δοίη.}$$

The recession of the Greek accent in the finite verb is accordingly everywhere not due to a process of accentual change within the word, but to a secondary accentuation which is a substitute for enclisis. It is false, therefore, to compare directly the accent of

[1] Εἰ and φής will be discussed further on.

finite forms with corresponding accent, *e. g.* in Sanskrit. **Thus, the accent** of δοίη is not to be compared with that of Sk. *deyāt*, but with ⌣ *deyāt, i. e.* the enclitic form; πεφύ(κ)αμεν not with *babhuvimá*, but with ⌣ *babhuvima;* Ζεὺς ὄρνυσι is Sk. *dyāús ṛṇoti* (the verb enclitic).

But in one respect the Greek enclisis of the finite verb has overstepped what was no doubt an old law accompanying it, a law which appears in the Vedic Sanskrit, cf. Whitney, Sk. Gramm. §591 fg. The Sanskrit verb *is inclined in independent paratactic clauses*, except when it stands at the beginning of a clause; the verb in hypotactic clauses, or at the beginning of a paratactic clause, etc., is orthotone. The Greek, it must be supposed, has forgotten and given up this original distribution of orthotonesis and enclisis, and has spread the analogy of the inclined forms over the entire finite verb.[1]

If the recessive accent of the Greek finite verb is regarded as a substitute for enclisis, then we can understand why the participles and infinitives are exempt from this accent with such perfect regularity. These forms were never subject to enclisis and have therefore retained their etymological accent in Greek undisturbed, even more so than noun-categories which stand in much looser relation to the finite verb; for these have often adopted the recessive accent. This result is obtained by comparing **Sk.** *bháran* with φέρων, *ricán* with λιπών, *ṛṇván* with ὀρνύς, *yán* with ἰών, *babhūván* with πεφυώς; so also λιπεῖν, λιπέσθαι, etc., which exhibit the same accent of the thematic vowel as in λιπών, have remained undisturbedly in the possession of their prehistoric etymological accent. In the same manner the accentuation of verbs compounded with prepositions is explained. The finite verb is inclined upon its preposition, *sám bhara* (written with tmesis in the Vedas) = σύμφερε, *ápi· asti* = ἔπεστι; on the

---

[1] It is interesting in this connection to mention that the enclisis of the Sanskrit verb had been regarded in the light of a prehistoric quality of I. E. speech much before Wackernagel; to be sure only in a casual mention. In a programme of the gymnasium at Wismar, 1869, there appeared a paper by Sonne entitled 'Zur ethnologischen Stellung der Griechen,' in which he writes: When we see that in Sanskrit the verb of the principal sentence is inclined upon every preceding 'objectiv-bestimmung,' we believe that we must recognize in this phenomenon, as strange as it is to our European conceptions, a remnant of proethnic accentuation (p. 3, cited by Delbrück, Sprachstudium, p. 132, note). He has in mind the coinciding enclisis of Greek εἰμι and φημι in making his statement, but he never extended his idea in any way beyond this mere suggestion.

other hand, here again the forms which are not enclitic when un-
compounded retain their accent, and the preposition loses its accent
both in Greek and Sanskrit, ὑπολαβών, ἐπιών; in the same manner
κάθηται and κατάκειται, but καθῆσθαι, κατακεῖσθαι, cf. Whitney, Sk.
Gramm. §1083.

Wackernagel turns next to the second persons εἶ and φῄς, which
are orthotone, and would endanger his entire explanation unless
their orthotonesis is explained. The explanation which is proposed
is a totally different one in each case.

For εἶ an etymological explanation is attempted. This word is
Attic and Ionic, but post-Homeric; it is a form, then, which is
later than the period in which the enclisis of the verb was fixed.
Possibly it may be restricted even to Attic alone, inasmuch as it
has been removed by Stein from Herodotus.[1] In order to explain
this late and contracted εἶ, Wackernagel assumes that it is a middle
form *ἔσεσαι to ἔσομαι. Such a word, containing as it does three
syllables, would, owing to the limitations of enclisis, not become
toneless, but would appear with recessive accent as a substitute for
enclisis in the usual way, and this *ἔ(σ)ε(σ)αι, *ἔεαι would then contract to εἶ, as *ποιέ(y)ε(σ)αι, ποιέεαι becomes ποιεῖ. But there are at
least two objections to this explanation. First, the natural explanation of εἶ, which seems to be almost unimpugnable, is a totally
different one. The word, whether restricted to Attic or not, is
evidently old; it is *ἔσι = Sk. dsi = Zd. ahi = Goth. is = Lithuanian esi and Old Bulgarian j-esi;[2] the assumption of a ground-
form *ἔσεσαι is therefore unnecessary and improbable. Secondly,
Wackernagel has assumed with indubitable success that within one
tense-system, forms which by themselves could have been enclitic
became recessive by the attraction of the rest of the system; why
has not the analogy of the enclitics in the paradigm of εἰμί succeeded
in overcoming this single recessive example in its turn? It seems
therefore much more probable that the lack of enclisis in εἶ is due
to the influence of contracted forms in general. At the time when
*ἔ(σ)ι contracted to εἶ, other contractions taking place at the same

---

[1] According to Veitch, Greek Verbs Irregular and Defective, Stein and Abicht
read εἶς, while Becker and Dindorf read εἶ.

[2] The Indo-European form of the second person singular was *esi, e. g. the
two s's coming together from the root es plus the -si of the second person singular
were simplified into a single s by some I. E. law of sound, before the separate
existence of the languages of the family. Neither in Greek nor in Sanskrit
would the theoretical *essi lose one of its s's. For the Sanskrit, see Whitney,
Sk. Gramm. §166.

time received the circumflex so generally that this form received it also, and was protected from the attracting influence of the enclitic paradigm, which it belongs to, by that same contract character.

The case of φής is quite a different one. Long monosyllabic finite **verbal** forms in Greek are regularly perispomena, that is, barytone or recessive; so βῆ, φῆ (or analyzed into morae, *βέε, *φέε); if this word does not receive the circumflex, it is **therefore not** accented recessively or quasi-enclitically, but is orthotone. Wackernagel ingeniously finds the cause of this orthotonesis in its peculiar function. 'A speaker never gets into the situation in which he speaks to another person about his (the other person's) φάναι **in the** present tense, without bringing the φάναι of that person into relation to something else, or otherwise when the φάναι of that person is still unknown to the speaker; in other words, grammatically expressed, φής occurs regularly in subordinate and interrogative sentences,' *loc. cit.* p. 461. That this rule is actually and not only theoretically true, Wackernagel then proceeds to show by bringing on all the passages in Homer and the tragedians in which the word occurs, p. 461–2, and his statistics bear him out completely.

The orthotonesis of this word in subordinate clauses is then identified with the regular orthotonesis of the verb in Vedic Sanskrit when it occurs in subordinate clauses (Whitney, Sk. Gramm. §595) and the orthotonesis in interrogative sentences, with a very similar rule for the Veda, according to which verbs in interrogative sentences retain their tone, or perhaps rather have their natural etymological tone, heightened still further by the rhetorical tone, natural in questions, cf. Whitney in Kuhn and Schleicher's Beiträge, I 200. It is clear that the criticism made above against the assumption that an old *ἐσεσαι which functionally was not different from ἐσμι should remain orthotone and resist the analogy of the rest of the forms of the paradigm does not hold good here, because there is a thoroughgoing functional difference in φής which might well hold it above the forces of assimilation; especially true might **this be** in the case of the peculiar interrogative tone, which this **word is subjected** to with especial frequency. In the later literature, as representatives of which Wackernagel brings on Plato and the comedians, this occurrence of φής in interrogative and subordinate clauses is not so strictly adhered to; he finds in 140 passages 18 not interrogative and not subordinate, but these passages are made **to** yield strong support to the correctness of his method in bringing on the Vedic accent for constant comparison; they also are explained by Vedic analogies. The word φῄς occurs in these 18 passages in the first one of two paratactic clauses, e. g. Plato Gorg. 491 B, σὺ μὲν γὰρ φῄς . . . ἐγὼ δὲ σοῦ τοὐναντίον. Compare with this Whitney, §596 : ' The verb of a prior (principal) clause is not infrequently accented in antithetical construction. Sometimes the relation of the two clauses is readily capable of being regarded as that of protasis and apodosis ; but often such a relation is very indistinct.'¹ Of course the Greek example comes under the head of antithetical construction ; in the same manner the other 17 examples of Plato, etc., are readily disposed of. It seems that Wackernagel has beyond peradventure pointed out the correct reason for the peculiarly isolated position of the word φῄς in accordance with the rules of Vedic and Indo-European accentuation.

He turns further to various minor specialties of the recessive and enclitic accent, and explains them again in accordance with well-known laws of Vedic accent. Only the most interesting of these, the orthotonesis of ἔστι, will be mentioned. The older Greek grammarians, according to Lehrs, Quaestiones epicae, p. 126, know of no functional difference between ἔστι and ⌣ ἐστι, but teach that the orthotone word stands at the beginning of the sentence and where certain particles, etc., immediately precede the word. According to some, only οὐ has this effect ; according to others οὐ, καὶ and ὡς ; εἰ, ἀλλά, and τοῦτο are also added by a few. With the exception of τοῦτο these words are either too weak to allow inclination upon them, or, like καί, are not real members of the sentence which they introduce, so that the ἔστι which follows stands in reality at the beginning of the sentence. This peculiarity is again explained by a rule in Whitney's Sk. Grammar, §593, 'The verb of a principal clause is accented when it stands at the beginning of the clause,' e. g. syáma íd índrasya çármaṇi, 'may we be in Indra's protection.'

Other details of Greek accentuation, which need not be repeated here, are successfully explained, and everywhere Wackernagel's results are strictly in accordance with the principles which have been stated above for all kinds of phonetic investigation, and they are themselves new proof of the success of such investigations when carried on with these principles. In the first place every line of his investigation is permeated with the thought that it is not allowable to discuss the accent of the separate I. E. language without

¹E. g. prá-prā 'nyé yánti, pary anyá āsate: 'some go on and on, others sit about.'

42

taking for a basis the reconstructed I. E. accent. Further, this I. E. accent could only change by regular phonetic law or by analogy. Both factors are shown to have been at work. The phonetic law is the Greek law of enclisis by which real historical enclitics appear accented, though in manner clearly enough a mere compensation for enclisis; the reason for this phonetic law lies within the province of phonetics just as, *e. g.* the rhotacism which changes in so many languages an *s* to an *r*.

The workings of analogy we saw in many ways; above all this, that the enclitic character of the verb in principal clauses has been extended to the verb in subordinate clauses. It would be interesting in this connection to count the number of principal and subordinate clauses in Homer; no doubt the principal clauses would preponderate, as they most certainly do in the Rig-Veda. Wackernagel is the first one who has clearly established any kind of law as regards the sentence-accent of the I. E. languages, the leading fact being the enclisis of the finite verb in principal clauses. His results prove completely the fact that the study of accent cannot be carried on from the point of view of the word alone, but that it must also consider the larger speech unit, the sentence, and perhaps ultimately also the smaller, the syllable.

Wackernagel does not carry his results beyond the finite verb, but he leaves no room for doubt that the nominal accent in Greek, so far as it is not archaic and etymological, is enclitic and recessive. No doubt the noun has to a large extent followed the verb in its enclisis; the Vedic accent leaves us here almost entirely, but yet not altogether. In the Veda the vocatives are accented only when they stand at the beginning of a sentence, or clause, or verse, elsewhere they also are enclitic; see Whitney, Sk. Gramm. §314, and Haskell in the Journal of the American Oriental Society, Vol. XI, p. 57 fg. Further, an adjective or genitive qualifying a noun in the vocative constitutes as far as accent is concerned a unity with it. Thus there arises in the case of a vocative in the middle of a clause a group of two or three, sometimes even more, unaccented nouns, cf. above, p. 11, note 2. The quantity of enclitic vocative material cannot have been very great at any period in any language of the family, yet it may have at least helped on the analogy of the verb in its inroads upon the noun. Possibly future investigations may succeed in pointing out the details of this process in an acceptable manner.

MAURICE BLOOMFIELD.

www.ingramcontent.com/pod-product-compliance
Lightning Source LLC
Chambersburg PA
CBHW021559270326
41931CB00009B/1295